Kitchen Secrets

Tips & Tricks Professional Chefs Don't Want You To Know

René Blanc

For Mim

Contents

It's Not Rocket Science

Soup Meet Cheese Rind

Give It a Rest

Spring, Summer, Autumn, Winter

Taste

Pastry Is Science

Clean As You Go

Control Your Heat

Relax, Cook, Repeat

1

Mise En Place

"Mise-en-place is the religion of all good line cooks. His carefully arranged supplies of sea salt, rough-cracked pepper, softened butter, cooking oil, wine, backups, and so on." Anthony Bourdain

Good mise is in the DNA of a professional chef. It is the fall back and it is the safety net. Time and time again it will save you from the brink of kitchen oblivion.

It means set in place, and it refers to the process of having your ingredients, preparation & equipment setup and ready to go *before* things get past the point of no return. In service this can mean having enough confit garlic roasted and sitting in extra virgin olive oil, or all of your seabass filleted and pin boned. Knowing where your backup chicken jus is *just incase* you run out of your first lot, or even having enough spoons to hand.

For you it can be as simple as chopping your onions, celery and carrot *before* you start the soup or checking you have enough cream and butter *before* you decide to make mashed potatoes.

Peeler / Spatula / Grater

These three utensils will save you lots of time and effort over the years. Buy high quality equipment and utensils, in the long run, it always pays off. A good quality speed peeler will make a world of difference and make peeling all your vegetables a breeze. A heat resistant plastic spatula and a sharp box grate will see you well and get you out of many tricky kitchen situations

3

Good Butter, Oil & Salt

Don't make your hollandaise with bad butter, it will taste bad. Don't make your vinaigrette with bad olive oil, why? it will taste bad. Don't season your fillet of bream with bad salt, because guess what, it will taste bad.

It's probably not unfair to say we could all benefit from having a little less butter, oil and salt in our diets. But it is, generally speaking, what makes most restaurant food taste so amazing. The hairs on the back of your neck would stand up on end if you saw how much butter a chef uses to finish their beurre blanc, how much salt goes into their cauliflower puree or even how much oil is used to dress your side salad.

When finishing a risotto at home, why waste the calories on bad butter? Slice off a big fat chunk of normandy butter and stir it in, your risotto will thank you. Been to the farmers market and bought incredible plum tomatoes? Smother them in italy's finest cold pressed extra virgin olive oil and when they're all gone mop up the juices with some fresh sourdough. Sprinkle some real sea salt flakes on top of your fudge sundae and worry about your sodium levels tomorrow.

Life is too short for bad butter, oil and salt.

4

Prep, Prep & More Prep

The devil is in the details. The details in a kitchen are in the preparation. The thing you hear most frequently being asked, shouted and uttered in a professional kitchen is "how is the prep looking?". Its different from your mise en place, its bigger, if the mise en place is the mortar then the prep is the bricks.

Without good prep a service can go sour in seconds. The simplest of tasks become near impossible in service, trying to make a hollandaise as you are searing steaks, trying to roll pasta as you are plating up desserts.

At home good prep can be as simple as whipping cream before you bake the cake or as advanced as cooking off your risotto rice a little before you cook it to order at your dinner party. Having a couple of containers of items you have prepared before hand takes the pressure off, meaning you can come home for work and have a quick dinner, or chat with guests at a dinner party rather than slave away in the kitchen.

5

Stick It Down

This one doesn't really hit home until you've seen a chef's finger tips left rolling around on their chopping board as they are carted off to hospital.

Put a damp cloth underneath your chopping board to stop it moving around as you chop and slice. Save yourself a trip to the emergency room to get those fingers sewn back on.

No Lid? Plastic Wrap

New pans, old lids, borrowed or stolen, lost or broken, chances are you have lots of odds and ends floating around in your cupboards and nothing fits quite right.

This is the bane of a chef's like. There are never enough lids, *ever*. The easy way around this, although it has to be said not exactly the safest, is to plastic wrap the top of your pan tightly. Now I must stress that if you are doing this at home, please poke a hole in your plastic wrap to allow the steam to escape, otherwise, BOOM.

Clothes Not Mitts

Oven mitts are a BAD idea. They trap your hands inside what can be a very dangerous situation. If you spill scalding hot oil on a pair of oven mitts with your hands inside chances are you aren't going to be able to get them off in time to save yourself from a serious burn.

Always use a thick cloth when handling hot pans. If an accident does happen then you can let go of the cloth straight away and save yourself from a bad burn.

Pass It

Pass everything through a sieve. Pass your soup through a sieve and mash your mashed potatoes through a sieve. Pour your gravies, stocks and reductions through a sieve. Rub your purees through a sieve. Sieve your flours through a sieve. Wash your rices and lentils then drain and toss them in a sieve.

No bits. Smooth. Remove impurities. That is the name of the game. A tomato soup with bits of skin that stick to your teeth is not a good soup. A veal reduction with bits of bone floating in it is not a good sauce. A cheesecake with clumps of icing sugar exploding in your mouth is not a good cheesecake.

It's a small extra step that goes a long way. Everytime you pass something you are automatically a better cook than those that don't.

Reduce, Constantly

Reduction intensifies flavour. This and good stock are the fundamentals of good sauce. Reduce until you have the amount you need then season just before serving, you can even 'mount' your sauce just before serving by whisked a couple of cubes of good butter through it , making it rich and luxurious.

It's better to have a little of something good than a lot of something bad.

Reduce a bottle of red wine with the same amount of good beef stock until you have a couple of spoonfuls left, you won't find a better sauce in any restaurant on the planet.

Take Stock

Good stock is the basis of great food. Chefs want to make you think stock is hard, they want you to believe it takes something *really special* to make good stock.

It doesn't.

You can make stock out of anything. The water that chickpeas have been soaking overnight in makes incredible vegetable stock. A leftover chicken carcass boiled in enough water to cover it makes amazing chicken stock. Beef bones roasted ferociously then simmered gently for a few hours makes the best beef stock. A couple of fish heads and a half lemon gently boiled for twenty minutes makes beautiful fish stock.

Whatever you have, throw it in a pan with water then boil, skim and drain. That's your stock.

Of course you can get as complicated as you like, you can add different varieties of bones, vegetables of all kinds to accentuate flavours, skim off impurities for hours, never let the temperature exceed a certain point, clarify through muslin cloth, add bouquet garnis, and all of that is fine, but good stock is just that, good stock. And it will transform your food.

Garnish

Garnish, to describe it bluntly, is a small amount of food used to decorate another food. But it can be a whole lot more complicated than that and it can be used to add texture, flavour, colour, smell, excitement, flair, intrigue, wonderment and most importantly, cost.

What sounds better?

Butternut Squash Risotto 12.95

Or

Butternut Squash Risotto
w/ toasted pumpkin seeds, herb feta, beetroot oil, crispy sage
18.95

Of course the garnish adds flavour and texture, and visually it looks a lot more appealing, but does that garnish equal a six dollar increase? It costs pennies and is all put on the dish at the last minute cold, meaning it doesn't take any extra work to produce. This is what separates the good restaurants from the bad, the home cook from the restaurant chef.

Knowing when and how to garnish food comes with experience and knowledge, but it is something you can easily start to incorporate into your adventures in cooking at home. Finish roasted vegetables with toasted nuts. Deep fry herbs to add to salads. Sautee breadcrumbs with garlic to finish pasta dishes. Whip cheese with a little oil to spoon over soups, finish cookies and cakes with popping candy.

The world of garnish is endless and full of infinite possibilities to liven up your dishes.

Season Little & Often

"My general advice to home cooks is that if you think you have added enough salt, double it."
Grant Achatz

Don't ever season all at once right at the end. You should be using little pinches of salt to season each separate stage of the cooking process.

Sweating off the onions? Pinch of salt. Adding the carrots and leek? Pinch of salt. Pouring in the vegetable stock? Pinch of salt. Blitzing with a stick blender? Pinch of salt. Splash of cream and a few cubes of cold butter? Pinch of salt.

By seasoning along the way you give the ingredients the opportunity to offer the best of themselves, you take that away from them by haphazardly dumping a couple of spoonfuls of salt on top, smothering them right before you sit down to eat.

Acidity

Acidity is a weapon lacking from most home cooks arsenal. A squeeze of fresh lemon will do wonders for nearly every dish, helping to make the flavours stand out from each other and sing a little more loudly.

A splash of vinegar can cut through a really rich sauce, whipped cream is another beast altogether with a squeeze of lemon.

Acidity should be used like salt, as another way to season your dishes.

14

Balance

Good cooking is all about creating balanced, harmonious food. Flavours, textures and ideas that compliment one another, that play off each other. You must think about balance constantly.

Is this dish to rich? Is it to sour? Or is it lacking a certain texture? Does the idea even work? You must ask yourself these questions constantly in order to address balance.

Brine

Ever wonder why the meat in restaurants is always so tender and juicy? Brining is the answer and it can help enhance juiciness in several ways.

Brining is the process of submerging a cut of meat in a brining solution, salt dissolved in water usually, and then leaving it for a set amount of time. The meat absorbs extra liquid resulting in a juicer end result, and absorbs salt which helps season the meat all the way through rather than just on the surface.

Brining is perfect for lean cuts of meat that can dry out during cooking.

Basic brine :
225 grams salt
+
3.75 litre water
=
Brine for 2.5 kilo of meat

6 - 12 hours

Umami

Umami is one of the five basic tastes, along with sweet, sour, bitter and salt. It is the secret weapon to creating full and deep flavour. Umami has a mild but lasting aftertaste that is difficult to describe. It induces salivation and a sensation of furriness on the tongue, stimulating the throat, the roof and the back of the mouth.

Foods rich in umami include ripe tomatoes, cured meat and fish, aged cheese and mushrooms.

Buy yourself some umami paste and brush it onto meat and fish, or add it to soups, stocks and sauces. People will be asking you for your secret ingredient.

It's Not Rocket Science

"The only real stumbling block is fear of failure. In cooking you've got to have a what-the-hell attitude."

Julia Child.

It's not as hard as it looks and it's definitely not as hard as chefs want you to think. Like any skill it will improve over time with practice. The more mistakes you make now the less you will make those same mistakes in the future.

To "julienne your carrots then saute gently, finishing with a napee of beurre noisette" just means fry thinly sliced carrots gently, then spoon over a little butter that you have browned in the same pan.

Forget about the lingo and jargon and just concentrate on what matters, the cooking. If a recipe seems too complicated then simplify it, if you are missing an ingredient then substitute it, don't get bogged down in semantics and lose faith. Cooking well is about having a natural instinct, an ability to follow your reactions on the fly.

In service things go wrong all the time, you may have ran out of certain ingredient, your fridge may be down, you might have cut off your index finger, but you always find a way through. We aren't trying to fry a spaceship to the moon, we are just trying to cook and serve tasty food.

18

Soup Meet Cheese Rind

The secret ingredient to any good soup. Parmesan rind. Dont throw it away, keep it and collect them, then add them to your soups for a huge hit of umami richness.

Give It a Rest

Rest your meat for half as long as you cook it. It won't go cold, if it does, that's what sauce is for. If you flash fry a iron steak for 5 minutes, rest it for 2 1/2 . If you roast a chicken for 2 hours, rest it for an hour. It's not a myth, apart from buying high quality produce resting your meat is the most important step in cooking like a real chef.

Spring, Summer, Autumn, Winter

"There is something deeply, unshakably right about eating food in season: fresh runner beans in July, grilled sardines on a blisteringly hot August evening, a bowl of gently aromatic stew on a rainy day in February." Nigel Slater. The Kitchen Diaries

Learning to cook and eat with the seasons can take a lifetime. It's a skill you need to let evolve naturally, over time. The produce looks and taste better, it's when it *wants* to be eaten. It's better for the environment & the planet, helps cut down on food miles and emissions.

Tender green asparagus, bright red apples, luminous yellow courgettes & dark, sinister cabbages, these are all meant to be eaten at certain times of the year.

21

Taste

Taste everything all the time. There is no simpler way to put it. You can learn so much about good cooking from just tasting.

 Taste good things and bad things, weird things and smelly thinks, things that you don't want to taste and things that you will never taste again, just taste them all. Each time you do you learn something about the produce, the chef, the time of year, the season.

Pastry Is Science

Cooking is art but pastry is science. Stick to the recipe and don't deviate.

Weigh everything, even your eggs. Get a good oven thermometer and use it, don't trust your dials. Use a real timer.

Think about it like a scientist, there should be no extra flourishes or off the cuff ideas when learning how to bake. Mastering the basics is essential, the creativity can come later when you understand the fundamentals of how pastry works.

Clean As You Go

Everything has a place. Be organised. Have a bowl in front of you at all times that your rubbish goes into, get rid of it before you move onto the next thing.

Giving your mind time to process what is happening is such an important part of working in a busy kitchen, this is why cleaning as you go makes or breaks you.

24

Control Your Heat

One of the most common mistakes home cooks make is the fear of the flame. If your pan is too hot, pick it up and move it off the heat, it's as simple as that, nothing to worry about.

Stop using cold pans, get your pans hot and learn to cook in them the way they are meant to be cooked in.

25

Relax, Cook, Repeat

"Cooking is a philosophy, it's not a recipe."

Marco Pierre White.

Stay relaxed, enjoy the time in the kitchen and have fun. pour a glass of wine, put some music on and open the windows.

Creating and eating wonderful food, whether it be alone or with friends and family, is something special and to be cherished. Savour the time spent cooking like you savour the food that ends up on the plate and table.

Printed in Great Britain
by Amazon

14122769R00021